CONSECRATION
TO THE
IMMACULATE HEART
OF MARY

Consecration P. 33

Immaculate Heart of Mary,
pray for us now and at the hour
of our death.

CONSECRATION
TO THE
IMMACULATE HEART OF MARY

According to the Spirit of
St. Louis De Montfort's
True Devotion to Mary

By

Father Nicholas A. Norman

Director of the Confraternity of
Mary Queen of All Hearts

TAN BOOKS AND PUBLISHERS, INC.
Rockford, Illinois 61105

Nihil Obstat: John J. Clifford, S.J.
                  Censor Deputatus

Imprimatur: ✠ Samuel Cardinal Stritch
                  Archbishop of Chicago
                  January 14, 1949

First published in 1949 by J. S. Paluch Co., Inc., Chicago.

Retypeset and published in 1988 by TAN Books and Publishers, Inc. The typesetting of this booklet is the property of TAN Books and Publishers, Inc., and may not be reproduced, in whole or in part, without permission in writing from the publisher.

ISBN: 0-89555-342-2

Library of Congress Catalog Card No.: 88-50839

Printed and bound in the United States of America.

TAN BOOKS AND PUBLISHERS, INC.
P.O. Box 424
Rockford, Illinois 61105

1988

PREFACE

With the wealth of devotions recommended to the faithful, many people become confused. They do not see the forest because of the leaves. They may lose sight of true devotion in the pursuance of certain external practices. They may take one leaf and say: "This is the forest." They may be ardently attached to a devotion to Our Lady under one title, such as Mother of Sorrows, Mother of Perpetual Help, Our Lady of Fatima, and disparage any other, thereby paying homage to the name rather than to the person, who is identical no matter what the appellation.

The truly devout see that all the leaves belong to the forest; that there is only one Immaculate Mother of God, and many external practices in her honor, many requests of hers lovingly to be obeyed. They seek the person beyond all the titles, and render to her real and true devotion.

This little book is intended to present briefly and simply the essence of true devotion, and an admirable and sure way of rendering that service to the Immaculate Queen. It describes a devotion simple in nature, but all-embracing in its possible external manifestations.

May the words of this book draw many to an ever-growing love for Our Lady, a love that will be unwearied in seeking to extend her reign over the hearts of men!

THE AUTHOR

ABBREVIATIONS
USED IN THIS BOOK

T.D.—*True Devotion to the Blessed Virgin Mary** (also called *True Devotion to Mary*), by St. Louis De Montfort.

S.M.—*The Secret of Mary*, by St. Louis De Montfort.

G.M.—*The Glories of Mary*,* by St. Alphonsus Liguori.

C.F.—*The Crusade of Fatima*, by Father John De Marchi.

R.R.—*Review for Religious*, May 1945.

S.A.—*The Soul Afire*, by H. A. Reinhold.

A.A.S.—*Acta Apostolica Sedis* (*Acts of the Apostolic See*) (July, 1947).

*Available from TAN Books and Publishers, Inc., P.O. Box 424, Rockford, IL 61105.

CONTENTS

Chapter 1

THE EMINENCE OF MARY

The Indictment of the
Modern World

We live in times that, whether they be the last days, or not, fulfill to a striking degree the words of St. Paul:

"Know also this, that in the last days, shall come dangerous times. Men shall be lovers of themselves, covetous, haughty, proud, blasphemers, disobedient to parents, ungrateful, wicked, without affection, without peace, slanderers, incontinent, unmerciful, without kindness, traitors, stubborn, puffed up, and lovers of pleasures more than of God: Having an appearance indeed of godliness, but denying the power thereof. . .ever learning, and never attaining to the knowledge of the truth." (2 Tim. 3:1-7).

"Lovers of themselves"—Let not the success of sundry charity drives blind us to the woeful spirit of selfishness that has gripped the world in its loveless embrace. "What is in it for me?"—this is the watchword of countless millions. Individuals are affected, and nations. So we have wars and the rumors of wars, the abominable housing situation, the grim, embattled strikes, ugly race prejudice, nervous impatience that explodes at the slightest delay in the fulfillment of personal desires, spiraling prices, a widespread breakdown of marriage, birth control and needless shuffling of child care to others, while so many mothers spend their time in activities of little or no value, or unnecessary em-

ployment, and so many fathers act as though their only
duty towards their children were to provide them with
material necessities and goods.

How many organizations, ostensibly high-minded and
charitable in purpose, are impeded in their efforts by
petty jealousies and cliques within their own ranks! Is
the spirit still dominant among us all as much as it was
among the first Christians, to unite for one purpose,
and for one alone—the glory of God and the extension
of His Kingdom?

"Human frailty," we say unctuously, and let it go at
that.

Once the pagans marveled, saying:

"See how these Christians love one another!"

They will say it today, but now with sardonic
amusement.

"Covetous"—Greed and avarice have wrecked the
modern world and prostrated civilization. What else
has caused wars, and so often lies beneath the high-
flown words of diplomacy?

"Haughty, proud, blasphemers"—For the first time
in history, while the majority may agree in theory that
there is a God, a vast proportion deny in practice the
existence of a Deity, and are gods unto themselves. Col-
leges of learning use His Name, but define Him fan-
tastically. His Name is not mentioned at the councils
of the nations. "Nature" has usurped His place as the
Author of Creation and the Arranger of its beautiful
order.

"Disobedient"—The revolt against the very idea of
authority exists not only in children, but has become
a real obsession in our age, an obsession which has
reached even into the fields of art and music, and is
responsible for the modern monstrosities, daubs and

cacophonies. To a staggering number, freedom means license, whether they wish to admit it or not.

"Without affection"—The world may have been as bad in pre-Christian times, but never since the Redeemer came and sanctified marriage has this exalted union been so abused, its promises so flouted. Never has personal desire counted for so much, and surrender for so little. Never has there been so little place in the world for children—birth control, abortion, neglect.

"Without peace"—The world is aflame with war, rumors of war, and revolt. Men cry "Peace, peace!"— but there is no peace.

"Slanderers"—"Propaganda" and "smearing" are common words now, and every child knows their meaning.

"Incontinent"—The world has been sexy in many periods of its existence. Prominent men have paraded their mistresses. But when since the times of ancient Rome has divorce been so legalized and shameless, with its attendant progressive polygamy? When was there such widespread birth control? When has the human body been paraded in such nudity? What stigma is attached to adultery and infidelity? Is it not "love"? And must not "love" be satisfied at any cost, regardless of encumbering husband, wife or children? What unprinted horrors are discovered by scratching the veneer of modern respectability! How often we read of the flame of lust raging in the hearts even of children, leading them to murder. Obscene pinups are commonplace in the rooms of teenagers. When was the world so flooded with pornographic writings and pictures, so many of which find their way into the hands of children? What age has seen such filthy advertisements, promising to reveal secrets of perversion, sexy comics, provocative motion pictures, dirty jokes sent into clean homes via radio?

The Romans adored Venus. Is she not being adored again?

But is not all this "broadminded" and "modern"? It is as broadminded and modern as Sodom and Gomorrah.

"Unmerciful"—Wandering refugees, wild children, slave labor, concentration camps nauseating in their horror, sadistic tortures that have shamed this decade forever and are still going on—these outrival the cruelties of the Huns and Mongols. And all this in a "civilized" world!

"Traitors"—When ever has the solid structure of the State well nigh universally been so shot through with the rat burrows of traitors working for another country, for foreign ideas and interests, covering their treason with the noble sounding cry of "Freedom, free speech, free press!" How many times in recent years has the enemy swallowed up a country without so much as firing a shot?

"Fifth columnists," "infiltration"—these are common household words today.

"Lovers of pleasures more than of God..."—no comment is needed.

"Ever learning and never attaining to the knowledge of the truth..." Our institutions of learning are bursting today as never before in history and they present numerous courses in widely varied fields. How many have for their object the education of man for the material concerns of life? How much time is allotted for the intensive cultivation of man's noble spirit?

To attain the truth means to find and to hold forever the Truth, the Infinite, Ineffable Essence. It calls not merely for a theoretical knowledge of the Divinity, but for *intimate union* with the All-Good, the All-Beautiful, the All-True.

Because so many have been so far from attaining the Truth, the foregoing indictment holds true. But those who have attained it have found the peace that surpasses all understanding.

ATTAINING THE TRUTH

In spite of all our troubles, we still speak of our era as "civilized times." We have automobiles, jet planes, streamlined trains, radio, television, plastics, the manifold applications and appliances of electricity, air conditioning, sanitation, penicillin, X-rays, and other as yet undreamed of wonders lie just beyond the horizon. They would soon be ours, if...

If...! If selfishness, misunderstandings, hatreds and fear were not draining the resources of mankind as we stand on the alert for cataclysmic war. Are we civilized?

What is civilization? Is it the existence in the world of such material marvels, really the product of only a comparatively few minds, or is it in the ability of all men to profit permanently by these things, as they free us from the burdens of earth to give us time and opportunity to achieve the sublime destiny of our immortal spirit?

Is civilization the pampering and the coddling of the senses, the making of life more comfortable, or is it the development of rugged character, that can live at peace with fellowman, while all try to perfect and ennoble the deathless spirit that places man at the pinnacle of all the visible creation?

Herein lies the indictment of our times, that we have gone pell-mell down the road of sense, and are making but desultory attempts to ascend the way of the spirit.

At the end of the low road of sense lies death,

corruption, and the stench of decay. At the heights of
the high road of the spirit awaits peace, and a joy immeasurable, beyond that of all our wistful dreams.

The road down is easy to sense, hard to spirit, in
its evergrowing disillusionment, emptiness and frightening desolation. The road up is hard to sense but easy
to the spirit, in the peace that surpasses all understanding.

At the dawn of reason we come to a parting of the
ways. Two roads lie ahead, one dipping slightly downward, the other sloping gently up. One is called Pleasure and one is called Truth. Neither is hard to follow,
though going up is more difficult than going down.
But they are not far apart, and it is easy to go from
one to the other.

But at adolescence comes a sharp turning. One leads
steeply upward, the other swiftly down. The latter,
though, is so broad, so smooth, so well-travelled; there
is so much to see, so much to do! Food, drink, pleasures abound, as far as the eye can see. The other road
seems so deserted, so narrow now and rocky, with dense
forest and long dark tunnels. So it is that many say:

"The roads have been marked wrong. It is on the
wide road that I shall find my joy and my fortune.
Can all these people walking it be making a mistake?"

So they start down, merrily sure. At first they see
many a lane marked "To Truth," but pass them by. The
slope becomes steeper, the momentum increases. There
are still roads over to Truth, but they are fewer now,
their markings hardly distinguishable. But after a while
food and drink begin to lose their appeal, and the pleasures to dim. Uneasiness grips the heart. Downward,
downward. Ever easier to go down, ever harder to go
back. Faster, faster, as the night comes on, until in the
darkness the false road ends at a precipice, and with

a despairing cry they plunge into the abyss. This is the story of every lost soul.

What shall take away the fear and the loneliness of the other path? There will be no fear in the company of a sure guide, one who has traversed every step of the way, has been through every dark tunnel and frightening wood, one alert and strong enough to repel every danger, one who knows every step of the way unto the very heights. There will be no loneliness if that guide be a friend, loved with all the power of our heart, and loving even more in return. Love makes all things easy, and the miles will pass away unnoticed. *"For though I should walk in the midst of the shadow of death, I will fear no evils, for thou art with me."* (Ps. 22:4). No fear, no tedium, no heartache, no desire to leave our Beloved to join the mocking throng. *"My beloved to me, and I to him."* (Cant. 2:16). This is all that is needed to make the going easy, and the final arrival sure.

There is only one under Our Lord among all the children of men who can fulfill perfectly the place of guide and beloved, only one with complete experience and complete love—the Immaculate Virgin. She has explored the way unto the Truth, and attained Him in a measure that no one else ever will or can. She has known all the darknesses that lead unto the light, the depths of suffering that has richly merited her the title of Queen of Martyrs. She alone of all mankind knows the fullness of the glory and the inexpressible joy that awaits at the end of the road. And her beauty is so compelling, and her love so selfless and divine, that if we but lift our eyes unto her we shall love her ardently in return and never wish to be separated from her. And if we but give her our hand, in complete trust, she will guide us safely to the Goal of All Desire.

So those whom she has guided and who have found

Him, call to us with all possible loving urgency: "Go to Mary!"

WE MUST FIND MARY

"In me is all grace of the way and of the truth, in me is all hope of life and of virtue." (*Eccles.* 24:25). In her we shall find the grace to attain unto Him who is the Way, the Truth and the Life.

To attain unto the Truth as the Apostle would have us do, we must first find Mary. To find Mary means to be united in intimate communion with her. This necessity is not intrinsic, but the Eternal Father has freely willed it that way and no other. Who shall say Him nay?

How do we know that the Father wants it that way? To understand this we must know something of Our Lady's place in the divine economy of salvation. This is something not too clearly understood by many Christians.

THE EXCELLENCE OF MARY

To understand her, we must first comprehend how God has endowed His Queen, how He has adorned her with matchless beauty and loveliness, irresistible power and ineffable glory.

St. Augustine says that whatever we may say in praise of Mary is little in comparison with what she deserves (*G. M.* p. 92). Pope Pius IX in defining the doctrine of the Immaculate Conception says that her sanctity exceeds that of all the Angels and Saints put together, and that it is so great that only the mind of God can comprehend it. (Papal Bull of Pius IX *Ineffabilis Deus*). St. Thomas Aquinas says: "From the fact that she is the Mother of God, the Blessed Virgin has a certain infinite dignity, derived from the Infinite Good who is God, and on this account cannot be anything better,

just as there cannot be anything better than God."
(*Summa Theol.* la. qu. 25 art. 6, ad. 4).

The only thing great enough to be compared with
Mary is number itself.

Number is not infinity. The bounds of number are
lost in mystery, but an immeasurable void separates it
from infinity. It is intrinsically impossible to imagine
anything being added to infinity. Number however is
capable of indefinite increase. Let us imagine the greatest
number we can comprehend—more can always be
added to it. Indeed we can multiply it by itself, cube
it, raise it to any power. Human understanding falters
and fails to grasp even comparatively low numbers; only
the mind of God can comprehend it all.

So with the perfections and the glory of Mary. She
is not infinite; a boundless chasm yawns between her
perfections and those of God. But her perfections are
as vast as number, and only the mind of God will ever
comprehend them.

Why did God endow her so? Can we give all His
reasons? *"Who has known the mind of the Lord, or
who has been His counsellor?"* But when we understand the nature of the objective and the subjective
redemption, we begin to see a gleam of light.

By His sufferings and death, Our Lord filled the infinite reservoir of divine grace. This was the objective
redemption.

To the Holy Spirit we attribute the work of dispensing these graces, of sending the limpid waters down
upon the parched desert and making it bloom. This
is the subjective redemption, and it is still going on.

The Divinity does not do this by Itself alone. God asso-
ciated a human being with Him so closely that the nearest
comparison in this world is the union of marriage,

wherein two, retaining their individual natures in a sense, become one. This one He called His spouse, and gave to her the administration of all the graces, so that she grants the divine largesse *"to whom she wills, as much as she wills, as she wills and when she wills."* (*T. D.* 25). She became the Mediatrix of All Graces, Spouse of the Holy Spirit, Queen of the Angels, Queen of Heaven and Earth.

Her position is unique in dignity and power. Her word is sufficient to draw down all graces. But neither does she work alone. St. Robert Bellarmine says that if Christ is the Head of the Mystical Body, then she is the neck through which everything passes from the Head to the rest of the body. The rest of the Mystical Body, by their sufferings, prayers, love and atonement, have a subordinate part in drawing down the waters from the reservoir. So it will be until the end of time. When the last grace has been given to the last man according to the eternal Divine Plan, then the Mystical Body will be complete, the Redemption will be accomplished not only objectively but also subjectively, and the new Creation will begin.

It is by accomplishing the subjective redemption, the drawing down and the application of the infinite merits of Christ, and dispensing them to mankind, that the work of the Head is completed by the rest of the Body, and the words of St. Paul are fulfilled: *"I fill up those things that are wanting to the sufferings of Christ."* (*Col.* 1:24). It is in the sense of the subjective redemption also that St. Augustine says:

"And so the Passion of Christ is not in Christ alone, and yet the Passion of Christ is in Christ alone. For if in Christ you consider both the head and the body, then Christ's Passion is in Christ alone, but if by Christ you mean only the head, then the Passion of Christ is not in Christ alone...Hence if you are members of Christ...whatever you suffer at the hands of those who are not members of Christ, was lacking to the sufferings of Christ. It is added precisely because it was lacking. You fill up the measure; you do not cause it to overflow. You will suffer just so much as must be added of your sufferings to the complete Passion of Christ, who suffered as our Head, and who continues still to suffer in His members, that is, in us. Into this common treasury each pays what he owes, and according to each one's ability, we all contribute our share of suffering. The full measure of the Passion will not be attained until the end of the world." (S. A. p. 219).

MARY MEDIATRIX OF ALL GRACES

Some say that Our Lady participated in the objective redemption, but this is not certain. At any rate, her preeminence in the work of the subjective redemption amply justifies her beautiful title: Co-Redemptrix (R. R.).

Mary is Mediatrix of All Graces in virtue of her ineffable union with her Spouse, the Holy Spirit, the Dispenser of All Grace.

What does this mean and what does this imply? Fr. Motherway, S.J. explains this clearly:

"Our Lady is Mediatrix in the sense that no petition of man can come to Christ except through her, also no grace or favor comes from Christ except through Mary. . . She is the one member of Christ's Mystical Body who mediates between the Head and the members, helping to apply to every one of them the very least gift that flows from the Head to every least member of that Body. . . No prayer to God or His Saints ever gets a hearing at the Throne of Infinite Majesty unless offered for us by the Queen of Heaven herself." (R. R.).

CONFIRMATION OF THIS DOCTRINE

The Saints abound who have extolled the extraordinary position and glory of Mary.

Witness these statements of Doctors of the Church:

St. Bernard—"God has filled Mary with all graces, so that men may receive by her means, as by a channel, every good thing that comes to them." (*G. M.* 93).

St. Alphonsus—"We most readily admit that Jesus Christ is the only Mediator of justice, and by His merits obtains for us all graces and salvation; but we say that Mary is the Mediatrix of Grace, and that, receiving all that she obtains through Jesus Christ, and because she prays for it and asks for it in the name of Jesus Christ, yet all the same, whatever graces we receive, they come to us through her intercession." (*G. M.* p. 90).

St. Bonaventure—"Mary is called 'the Gate of Heaven' because no one can enter that blessed Kingdom without passing through her." (*G. M.* 94).

St. Robert Bellarmine—"God decreed that all the gifts, all the graces, and all the heavenly blessings which proceed from Christ as the Head should pass through Mary to the Body of the Church. Even as the physical body has several members in its other parts, but only one head and neck, so also the Church has many Apostles, Martyrs, Confessors and Virgins, but only one Head, the Son of God, and one bond between the Head and the members, the Mother of God." (Concio 42, *De Nativitate B. V. M.*).

As for the other Saints, let St. Louis De Montfort, the herald of Mary, speak for them all:

"We have three steps to mount to God: the first, which is nearest to us, and most suited to our capacity, is Mary; the second is Jesus Christ, the third is God the Father. To go to Jesus, we must go to Mary; she is the Mediatrix of intercession." (*T. D.* 86).

"To Mary, His faithful spouse, God the Holy Ghost has communicated His unspeakable gifts. He has chosen her to be the dispenser of all He possesses, in such sort that she distributes to whom she wills, as much as she wills, as she wills and when she wills, all His gifts and graces. The Holy Spirit gives no heavenly gift to men which He does not pass through her virginal hands. Such has been the will of God who has willed that we should have dioceses on May 31.

From the multitudinous testimonials of the Church to the glory of Mary, we mention but a few:

The Church applies to her the words of the *Book of Ecclesiasticus,* 24:5:

"In me is all grace of the way and of the truth; in me is all hope of life and of virtue."

Likewise from the *Book of Proverbs* 8:35:

"He that shall find me, shall find life, and shall have salvation from the Lord."

Leo XIII, in the encyclical of September 22, 1891:

"We may affirm that by the will of God, nothing is given to us without Mary's mediation, in such a way that just as no one can approach the almighty Father but through His Son, so no one, so to speak, can approach Christ but through His Mother."

Pius X, in the encyclical of February 2, 1904:

"By the communion of sorrows and of will between Christ and Mary, she has deserved to become the dispenser of all the blessings which Jesus acquired for us by His Blood."

Benedict XV authorized the Mass of Mary, Mediatrix of All Graces, celebrated in certain dioceses on May 31.

What is the theological rating of the proposition that Mary is Mediatrix of All Graces? Fr. Dennis Burns, S. J. writes thus:

"The strongest note that can be applied at present to the proposition that Our Lady is the Mediatrix of All Graces is *'de fide Catholica ex jugi magisterio fere proxime definibilis'* [of Catholic Faith from the universal teaching authority of the Church, just about ready for definition] since it has been generally accepted by the *'ecclesia docens et discens'* [the Church teaching and taught], vigorously proposed by St. Bernard and others, all the contrary arguments have been solved, but a little more time is required for a better understanding on the part of the faithful of the theological formula of the doctrine to be defined and for removing whatever practical microscopic doubts and difficulties there may be in the mind of some." It may be noted that such microscopic doubts and difficulties persisted about the Immaculate Conception until its definition, after which of course there was no longer any room for argument.

REASON FOR MARY'S POSITION

The ultimate reason for Mary's preeminence among the children of men is the will of God, who envisioned His spouse from all eternity and in time created her to His image and likeness with a fidelity of detail unknown to any other, and adorned her with His choicest graces.

But did Mary do anything of herself to merit for herself? Indeed she did.

Sanctity is the perfect alignment and welding of the human will with the Divine will. This Mary did to the most perfect degree possible.

All Heaven and earth waited for her consent for the Incarnation. And consent she did, knowing full well it would entail deep suffering on her part. Being full of grace, she was full of the gifts of the Holy Spirit; and the Spirit of Wisdom gave her to understand the prophecies. She saw no earthly monarch in the Messias, but the Sovereign of the Kingdom of God. She knew He would be *"despised, and the most abject of men, a Man of Sorrows"* (*Isaias* 53) and that His suffering would be her own.

She loved her Son as no other mother dare love her child; she could truly adore Him, for He was God. And when the time came for Him to bear upon Himself the sins of the world, His most exquisite agony, she understood and felt, more than anyone else in the world who ever was or will be, His excruciating suffering, for she too was sinless. When we love, it is harder to see the one we love suffer than it is to bear the sufferings ourselves. Yet her will remained steadfast, united to the will of the Father even in the face of the ultimate pain.

St. Robert Bellarmine writes:

"Have no doubts about it, the Blessed Virgin suffered extremely when she beheld her Son hanging on the gibbet of the Cross. But she loved the honor and glory of God more than the human flesh of her Son. She stood there under the Cross as the Valiant Woman who showed not the trace of impatience over the exquisite pains to which Christ was unjustly condemned. She did not fall to the earth, faint with grief, as some artists would have us believe; she did not tear her hair or scream or bewail as other women might, but bore her sorrow courageously, because she knew that the spectacle before her had been justly willed by God. As much as she loved the human form of Christ, she loved the honor of His Father and our Redemption more. Thus did she blend her own affections with those of Christ, who also preferred His Father's glory and our salvation to the temporal safety and security of His human body." (*De Septem Verbis Domini,* c. 11).

METHOD OF INTERCESSION

Mary obtains all graces for us by her infallible intercession.

St. Louis De Montfort writes:

"The authority which God has been well pleased to give her is so great that it seems as if she had the same power as God; and her prayers and petitions are so powerful with God that they always pass for commandments with His Majesty, who never resists the prayer of His dear Mother because she is always humble and conformed to His will." (*T. D.* 27).

Fr. Motherway says:

"How then does Mary dispense God's grace to us? Most theologians say that she dispenses by interceding, so that there is not a complete difference between her activity as intercessor and her activity as a dispenser of divine favors. But her intercession has a special character because of which it can be rightly called an act of distribution. If you ask what that characteristic is, we reply that such is the attitude of our Divine Lord, Mary's Son, towards His well-beloved Mother that He looks upon her every request as though it were a command. Hence for her to ask a favor is the same as to designate its recipient. Our Lord never refuses her prayer. He has determined never to do so, and in that sense He cannot do so; in Heaven, Mary's wish always prevails. Hence too it may be said that her intercession is infallible. It never fails." (*R. R.*).

NEED OF HER INTERCESSION

If Mary is the Mediatrix of All Graces, the need of her intercession for us and our complete union with her, is obvious.

St. Louis De Montfort observes:

"Mary has produced, together with the Holy Spirit, the greatest thing that has ever been or ever will be— the God-Man...It is only that singular and miraculous Virgin who can produce, in union with the Holy Spirit, singular and extraordinary things.

"When the Holy Spirit, her Spouse, has found Mary in a soul, He flies there. He enters there in His fullness; He communicates Himself to that soul abundantly, and to the full extent to which it makes room for His spouse. Nay, one of the great reasons why the Holy Spirit does not now do startling wonders in our souls is because He does not find there sufficiently great union with His faithful and inseparable spouse." (*T. D.* 36).

This is the glory of Mary—favorite daughter of the Father, Mother of the Son, Spouse of the Holy Spirit, Gate of Heaven, Mediatrix of All Graces, Queen of Heaven and Earth. And who shall list all the other titles of Her Majesty?

But there is one title that she still lacks—one to which she has every right, yet not one to be conferred upon her by the Eternal Father, but only by her children. It is the title that proclaims her reign over their free wills, their hearts. Loving us with a love beyond all the power of words to say, she yearns with inexpressible longing for that title which it is in our power, and only in ours, aided by grace, to give—"*Queen of All Hearts.*"

What shall we do that she may be given the crown of the Kingdom of the Hearts of Men?

We must simply render unto her, and see to it that as many as we can inspire to do the same shall likewise eagerly and joyously give unto her, True Devotion— not just anything that passes for devotion, but devotion in the truest, fullest sense, all that is in our power to give and to obtain for her.

Chapter 2
TRUE DEVOTION

Devotion is a much abused word. Shoddy imitations exist which usurp the place of the true in the hearts of many of the faithful. Sentimental stirrings and personal-interest motivated prayer often don the apparel of true devotion, and the spurious often crowds out the genuine. Abundance of words becomes more important than sincere love, warm but inefficacious feeling more desirable than arid will. Pursued, this course leads to our having to say some day:

"Master, we have labored all the night, and caught nothing."

There is nothing mysterious about true devotion. It is *love*, pure and simple. But love is love only insofar as it forgets pure self and becomes absorbed in the will, the good and the glory, and the embrace of perfect union, of the beloved. "*He must increase, and I must decrease*" (*Jn.* 3:30)—this is the expression born of true love.

So easy it is to see this in our human relations. The devoted husband is the one who seeks constantly to make his wife happy, disregarding his own desire for rest and personally appealing recreations. The devoted wife and mother works to the limit of human endurance with a light heart, finding her happiness in making her family happy.

Psychiatrists earnestly advise the ill to seek their happiness outside of themselves. Seeking themselves, they feed upon themselves. Seeking their happiness in the service of others, selflessly and without expectation of return, they find release, quiet, serenity and joy.

When these natural motives are sublimated to the supernatural, and we serve and love ultimately God, rather than allowing our efforts to terminate in ourselves and our fellow men, then we find *"the peace that surpasses all understanding."*

It should be evident that if the service of our fellow man rather than the seeking of self can bring deep contentment, then the loving service of God for His own sake should bring immeasurably more, for He is the All, the goal of all desire. But strange are the ways of man! What should be as clear as light does not in practice seem to be so evident at all, with the result that many say that they love God, but their regard is of a quality decidedly inferior to the kind they entertain for their fellow man. The creature, the imperfect— he receives true love; the Uncreated, the All-Beautiful, the All-Good, the All-True receives a makeshift imitation that would be angrily rejected were it offered to men.

So people curiously imagine that they love God when they seek Him only to get temporal gifts that will make the world more attractive and pleasing. How many would not go to any trouble at all, if they knew in advance that the temporal gift they are asking would not be granted, but a spiritual one of far higher value that would bring far closer union with the Lord, would be substituted in its place, and its delights would be known only in the world to come? How many, when they do receive, grab and run, without a word of thanks, with what in human relations would be considered shameless manners and outright boorishness.

True devotion is *love,* and love means:

"He must increase, but I must decrease." (Jn. 3:30).

True devotion will often, and in this mortal life usually, be mixed with adulterating self-love. One hundred percent true devotion is pure sanctity, rare indeed here below. But with thoughtful attention, desire and prayer we can ever refine our love, and make it more pleasing to God.

True love does not exclude our asking God for spiritual and temporal favors. Indeed, they must be asked for, always and without ceasing. But are we not then seeking self, the antithesis of true love?

There is no conflict, but only the necessary co-ordination of petition and love, when we seek only those things which will increase God's pleasure in us and our union with Him, and we reject all those things that would lessen His pleasure in us. In this way, all that we seek is for the greater honor and glory of God, and not for pure self at all. It is not then self we seek, but God.

True love is one; there are not different kinds of true love any more than there are different kinds of truth. True devotion to God is one, no matter what attribute we glorify. True devotion to Our Lady is likewise one, no matter under what title we honor her. Yet do we not sometimes hear people vigorously defending the devotion to Our Lady of Perpetual Help and disparaging, say, the devotion to Our Lady of Fatima? Or having complete faith in Our Lady of Sorrows, and but little in Our Lady of Mount Carmel or Our Lady of Lourdes?

Is this not childishness unworthy of an adult? Is Our Lady one or many? Is she her own rival?

All of these devotions are good, but all demand *true devotion.* This true devotion will seek Our Lady's good, glory and exaltation, and will look for gifts for self

only insofar as they will increase her joy in us, and
the honor and glory we can give and obtain for her,
and our union with her, for love is union. "Devotion"
which seeks self and this world alone is a sorry sort
of devotion, indeed!

There is only one light coming down from the sun.
But this light, touching the emerald, or the ruby, or
the diamond, gives to each its separate loveliness. Who
shall say which is more beautiful than the rest?

It may be well to utter here a word of caution regard-
ing an unwarranted assumption that is sometimes made
by those who follow or who have heard of St. Louis
De Montfort. Although he entitled his marvelous work
True Devotion to the Blessed Virgin Mary, he expressly
repudiated the idea that the practices therein outlined
constitute the only form of true devotion to Mary.

"There are several interior practices of true devotion
to the Blessed Virgin. Here are the principal ones, stated
compendiously: (1) To honor her as the worthy Mother
of God, with the worship of hyperdulia; that is to say,
to esteem her and honor her above all the other Saints,
as the masterpiece of grace, and the first after Jesus
Christ, true God and true Man; (2) to meditate on her
virtues, her privileges and her actions; (3) to contem-
plate her grandeurs; (4) to make acts of love, of praise,
of gratitude to her; (5) to invoke her cordially; (6) to
offer ourselves to her and unite ourselves with her; (7) to
do all our actions with the view of pleasing her; (8) to
begin, to continue and to finish all our actions by her,
in her, with her and for her, in order that we may
do them by Jesus Christ, in Jesus Christ, with Jesus
Christ and for Jesus Christ, our Last End...

"True devotion to Our Lady has also several exterior
practices, of which the following are the principal ones:
(1) to enroll ourselves in her confraternities and enter her
congregations; (2) to join the religious orders instituted

in her honor; (3) to proclaim her praises; (4) to give
alms, to fast and to undergo outward and inward mor-
tifications in her honor; (5) to wear her liveries, such
as the Rosary, the Scapular or the little chain; (6) to
recite with attention, devotion and modesty the holy
Rosary composed of fifteen decades of Hail Marys in
honor of the fifteen principal mysteries of Jesus Christ;
or five decades...or some other prayers, hymns and
canticles of the Church; (7) to sing, or have sung,
spiritual canticles in her honor; (8) to make a number
of genuflections or reverences... (9) to take care of her
confraternities, to adorn her altars, to crown and ornament her images; (10) to carry her images or have
them carried in procession, and to carry a picture or
an image of her about our own persons, as a mighty
arm against the evil spirits; (11) to have copies of her
name or picture made and placed in churches or in
houses, or on the gates and entrances into cities,
churches and houses; (12) to consecrate ourselves to her
in a solemn and special manner." (*T. D.* 115-116).

The followers of St. Louis commonly refer to the
practices, interior and exterior, of true devotion for
which he has a special predilection, as "The True
Devotion." This can give rise to misunderstandings, and
to the false assumption that the practices he advocates
are the *only* expression of true devotion.

There are many varieties of wine, some admittedly
more excellent than others, but they are all true wine.
There are varying degrees of true love of God, according to our willingness to forsake venial sin, inordinate
attachments and imperfections; so too there are varying degrees of true devotion to Mary.

St. Louis, having expressly stated that there are many
forms of true devotion, states his claims with regard
to the particular practices he advocates:

"But after all, I loudly protest that, having read nearly

all the books which profess to treat of devotion to Our
Lady, and having conversed familiarly with the best and
wisest men of these latter times, I have never known or
heard of any practice of devotion toward her at all equal
to the one which I now wish to unfold; demanding from
the soul, as it does, more sacrifices for God, emptying
the soul more of itself and of its self-love, keeping it more
faithfully in grace and grace more faithfully in it, unit-
ing it more perfectly and more easily to Jesus Christ; and
finally, being more glorious to God, more sanctifying to
the soul and more useful to our neighbor than any other
of the devotions to her." (*T. D.* 118).

But we shall refer to St. Louis De Montfort later,
and here continue to treat of true devotion in general.

True devotion is like the light of the sun. It touches,
or rather permeates, and floods with glory, devotion
to her under any title whatsoever, or by any approved
practices whatsoever. It is internal and intrinsic, and
can bear many external forms. It is the form that gives
life and vigor and substance to the prime matter of
external and internal practices. For true devotion is love,
and true devotion to Mary is simply the real and genuine love of Mary, delighting in every title that can be
bestowed upon her, glorying in their number, grieved
only by the efforts of those who would seek to narrow
their limits or to dim their brilliance.

Shall we limit the Queen to diamonds and deny her
emeralds, rubies, sapphires and pearls? Shall we limit
her to roses and deny her lilies and orchids?

Never let it be thought that true devotion is a new
devotion added to the galaxy, or that it limits anything.
It is as wide as love, for it is love, and delights in any
and every external expression of genuine affection for
our Queen Mother. It rejoices in the light from any
and all of the unnumbered facets of the Gem of God—
Mary Most Holy, ever a Virgin.

INTERNAL AND EXTERNAL DEVOTION

What good is gratitude, if it be not shown? What good is love, if no evidence is given of it, nor proof? What good is love that never shines forth in the brightness of a smile, the warmth of expression, the little sacrifices that sound forth with the glory of silver trumpets:

"Thus do I show that it is my will that thou shalt increase and I shall decrease!"

True interior devotion cannot, simply cannot, exist without external manifestation. "*Out of the abundance of the heart the mouth speaketh.*" (*Matt.* 12:34). But the reverse, alas, is not true. External devotion can exist without the internal, but when it does it is meaningless, a mockery, shoddy and worthless. "*This people honoreth Me with their lips, but their heart is far from Me.*" (*Matt.* 15:8). Do not some people pride themselves on being good Christians simply because they go to divine services with regularity and make donations, while most of the time they are in unrepented mortal sin, enemies of God, having evicted Him from their hearts? What monstrous kind of "devotion" is this?

Of such it is written:

"*Not every one that saith to me, Lord, Lord, shall enter into the Kingdom of Heaven; but he that doth the will of My Father who is in Heaven, he shall enter into the Kingdom of Heaven.*

"*Many will say to Me in that day: Lord, Lord, have we not prophesied in Thy Name, and cast out devils in Thy Name, and done many miracles in Thy Name?*

"*And then I will profess unto them: I never knew you; depart from Me, you that work iniquity.*" (*Matt.* 7: 21-23).

Must not all of us paraphrase the bitter lament of Cardinal Wolsey, and say:

"If I had served my God with half the love I served myself. . ."

True Devotion is the blindingly splendid spirit; let it enter and inform whatsoever bodies it will, and they shall be beautiful and glorious before the Lord.

Speak for Mary, act for Mary, honor her, glorify and extol her before men, and the spirit and the body shall be united, and stand before the Lord in wondrous beauty, and He shall look upon His handiwork, and see that it is good, and rest.

THE ULTIMATE END
OF ALL DEVOTION IS GOD

We must always retain true perspective in our devotions. Mary, great and ineffable as she is, is not the final vanishing point, the focus of all. No one would be so angry as she if we acted on this assumption. Devotion to Mary is not an end in itself. She is the Mediatrix with the Son, and He is the sole Mediator with the Father. It is not she who glorifies herself; it is the Father who glorifies her. It is the Eternal Father's free will that things be done this way. She is the way unto the Way, the truth unto the Truth, the life unto the Life.

St. Louis De Montfort is among the first to decry any abuse:

"Inasmuch as grace perfects nature, and glory perfects grace, it is certain that Our Lord is still, in Heaven, as much the Son of Mary as He was on earth, and that consequently He has retained the obedience and submission of the most perfect child toward the best of all mothers. But we must take great pains not to conceive this dependence as any imperfection or abasement in Jesus Christ. For Mary is infinitely below her Son, who is God, and therefore she does not command Him as a mother here below would command her child,

who is below her. Mary being altogether transformed
by God's grace, and by the glory which transforms all
the Saints into Him, asks nothing, wishes nothing, does
nothing, which is contrary to the eternal and immuta-
ble will of God. When we read then in the writing
of Sts. Bernard, Bernardine, Bonaventure and others,
that in Heaven and on earth, everything, even to God
Himself, is subject to the Blessed Virgin, they mean
that the authority which God has been well pleased
to give her is so great that it seems as if she had the
same power as God, and that her prayers and petitions
are so powerful with God that they pass for commandments with His Majesty, who never resists the prayer
of His dear Mother because she is always humble and
conformed to His Will." (*T. D.* 27).

St. Louis states as the first fundamental truth of the
True Devotion to Mary that "Jesus Christ is the last
end of devotion to Mary."

"Jesus Christ our Saviour, true God and true Man,
ought to be the last end of all our other devotions, otherwise they are false and delusive. Jesus Christ is the Alpha
and Omega, the beginning and end of all things. We
labor not, as the Apostle says, except to render every
man perfect in Jesus Christ, because it is in Him alone
that the whole plenitude of the Divinity dwells together
with all the other plenitudes of graces, virtues and perfections. It is in Him alone that we have been blessed
with all spiritual benediction; and He is our only Master, who has to teach us; our only Lord, on whom we
ought to depend; our only Head, to whom we must
be united; our only Model, to whom we should con-
form ourselves; our only Physician, who can heal us;
our only Shepherd, who can feed us; our only Way
who can lead us; our only Truth whom we must believe; our only Life who can animate us; and our only
All in all things who can satisfy us. There is no other

name given under Heaven except the Name of Jesus,
by which we can be saved. God has laid no other foun-
dation of our salvation, our perfection or our glory,
than Jesus Christ. Every building that is not founded
on that firm rock is founded upon the moving sand,
and sooner or later will infallibly fall. Every one of
the faithful who is not united to Him as a branch to
the stock of the vine, shall fall, shall wither, and shall
be fit only to be cast into the fire. Outside of Him
there exists nothing but error, falsehood, iniquity, fu-
tility, death and damnation. But if we are in Jesus Christ
and Jesus Christ is in us, we have no condemnation
to fear. Neither the angels of Heaven nor the men of
earth nor the devils of Hell nor any other creature can
injure us, because they cannot separate us from the
love of God, which is in Jesus Christ. By Jesus Christ,
in Jesus Christ, we can do all things; we can render
all honor and glory to the Father in the unity of the
Holy Ghost; we can become perfect ourselves, and be
to our neighbor a good odor of eternal life.

"If then, we establish solid devotion to our Blessed
Lady, it is only to establish more perfectly devotion
to Jesus Christ, and to provide an easy and secure means
for finding Jesus Christ." (*T. D.* 61).

And he expresses in a sublime prayer all that is to
be hoped for ultimately from true devotion:

*"Make me love Thee, my Lord, ardently, so that
I may obtain of Thy mercy a true devotion to Thy
Holy Mother, and inspire the whole earth with it;
and for that end receive the burning prayer which
I make to Thee, with St. Augustine and Thy other
true friends:*

*"Thou art Christ my tender God, my great King,
my good beautiful and my most beloved, my living
Bread, my Priest forever, my Leader to my country,
my True Light, my holy Sweetness, my straight Way,*

*my excellent Wisdom, my pure Simplicity, my pacific
Harmony, my whole Guard, my good portion, my everlasting salvation.*

"*Christ Jesus, my sweet Lord, why have I ever loved,
why in my whole life have I ever desired anything except Thee, Jesus my God? Where was I when I was
not in Thy mind with Thee? Now, from this time forth,
do ye, all my desires, grow hot, and flow out upon
the Lord Jesus; run, ye have been tardy this far; hasten
whither ye are going; seek Whom you are seeking.*

"*O sweet Jesus, may every good feeling that is fitted
for Thy praise, love Thee, admire Thee, delight in Thee.
God of my heart, and my portion, Christ Jesus, may
my heart faint away in spirit and mayest Thou be my
life within me! May the live coal of Thy love grow
hot within my spirit, and break forth into a perfect
fire; may it burn incessantly on the altar of my heart;
may it flow in my innermost being; may it blaze in
hidden recesses of my soul; and in the day of my con-
summation, may I be found consummated with Thee!
Amen.*" (*T. D.* 67).

FORMS OF TRUE DEVOTION

True devotion to Our Lady has one intrinsic
characteristic—*it leads through her to Jesus*. It may
have many external forms. None of these has a monopoly of true devotion. One may lead to Him by a more
direct route, one less direct; one may be easier, one
less easy; one may be more attractive to an individual
soul than any other form, but if a devotion to Our
Lady surely leads us to her Son, then it is true devotion.

Pope Pius XII, speaking to the pilgrims who attended
the canonization of St. Louis De Montfort, spoke thus:

"Now it is necessary to speak of sincere and loyal
devotion. He is the author of the treatise *True Devotion*

to the Blessed Virgin, which is distinguished by those very traits from a false devotion more or less superstitious, or from some superficial sentiments, which puts on the appearance while living in sin, counting on a miraculous grace at the last hour.

"True devotion, that of Tradition, that of the Church, that, We say, in a good Christian and Catholic sense, tends essentially to union with Jesus under the guidance of Mary. The form and practice of this devotion may vary according to times, places, personal inclinations. Within the limits of a sane, sure doctrine, of orthodoxy, and the dignity of the cult, the Church allows her children a just margin of liberty. Their conscience in regard to what is the true and perfect devotion towards the Holy Virgin is not at all so bound to these modalities that any one of them can claim a monopoly.

"Behold, therefore, beloved sons and daughters, why We ardently desire that, over and above the various manifestations of piety towards the Mother of God, Mother of Men, you may draw from the treasure of the writings and examples of our Saint, that which he made the basis of his Marian devotion:

> *his firm conviction of the most powerful intercession of Mary;*
> *his resolute will to imitate her as far as possible;*
> *the vehement ardor of his love for her and for Jesus.*" (A. A. S. 1947).

Those who glance over the surface of a devotion, without ever plumbing its depths, are like a man who sees a few flecks of gold lying on the ground, and calls himself rich, never going down to the fabulously rich vein below. Vain sentimentality can encourage many and curious external practices, but only *faith* and *love* can inspire the labor of mining the true treasure. And indeed the writings of St. Louis De Montfort are a treasure, as the Holy Father affirms, and in the vastness of its riches will be found the pure gold of *true devotion*.

ST. LOUIS DE MONTFORT

Louis Grignion was born at Montfort, France, on January 31, 1673, of well-to-do, influential parents. From his father, who was of the old, austere patriarchal type, whose word was absolute law, he inherited a stubborn determination, which however he used entirely to advance the reign of Jesus and Mary. He spurned the comforts and advantages of his inherited station in life, and offered himself to God completely in the priesthood. He was ordained in 1690, and so utterly did he break with his former world that he dropped his family name, and called himself simply "Louis of Montfort."

The going was rough for him all the days of his priesthood. In that powdered and perfumed age, he ignored the fastidious conventions of deportment and attire to such an extent that he alienated practically everyone who knew him. His times could not understand such complete detachment. His contemporaries lauded the Saints for similar lives, but when the reality was brought before their very eyes, it was a different matter. He was rejected, despised, contemned and condemned with an insistence that would have broken a lesser spirit. St. Paul speaks of those who were "...*in want, distressed, afflicted; of whom the world was not worthy*..." (Heb. 11:37-38). Louis of Montfort was one of these. But now, as the great mills of God grind on, slowly but exceedingly fine, Louis stands forth as St. Louis Marie Grignion de Montfort, a Saint, a canonized Saint.

He bequeathed to the world a treasury of gold and jewels, set in the casket of his treatise: *True Devotion to the Blessed Virgin Mary*. Let Father Faber, the great

English spiritual writer, speak of that sublime work:

"If I may dare to say so, there is a growing feeling of something inspired and supernatural about it, as we go on studying it; and with that we cannot help experiencing, after repeated readings of it, that its novelty never seems to wear off, nor its fullness to be diminished, nor the fresh fragrance and sensible fire of its unction ever to abate." (*T. D.*, preface).

One may imagine the fury of the Evil One as this book was being written. He does his utmost to cloud men's minds to its glories and truths, as he clouded the minds of the Scribes and Pharisees. The Saint prophesied this attack and foretold that his work would be lost awhile, as indeed it was, being rediscovered only in 1842.

St. Louis died at St. Laurent-sur-Sevre on April 28, 1716. On May 12, 1853, his doctrines were pronounced free from error. He was beatified by Pope Leo XIII in 1888, and canonized by Pope Pius XII on July 20, 1947.

HIS DEVOTION NOT NEW

At the outset, let it be said that St. Louis did not consider himself the originator of the doctrine he proposed and preached with all his soul. He expressly disclaims that honor.

"The practice which I am teaching is not new. M. Boudon, who died a short time ago in the odor of sanctity, says in a book which he composed on this devotion, that it is so ancient that we cannot precisely fix the date of its beginning. It is, however, certain that for more than seven hundred years we find traces of it in the Church." (*T. D.* 159 sq.).

ESSENCE OF HIS DEVOTION

He expresses the essence of his devotion in the following words:

"All our perfection consists in being *conformed, united and consecrated to Jesus Christ;* and therefore the most perfect of all devotions is, without any doubt, that which the most perfectly conforms, unites and consecrates us to Jesus Christ. Now, Mary being the most conformed of all creatures to Jesus Christ, it follows that of all devotions, that which most consecrates and conforms the soul to Our Lord is devotion to His holy Mother, and that *the more a soul is consecrated to Mary, the more it is consecrated to Jesus.*

"Hence it comes to pass that the *most perfect consecration to Jesus Christ is nothing else but a perfect and entire consecration of ourselves to the Blessed Virgin,* and this is the devotion which I teach; or, in other words, a perfect renewal of the vows and promises of holy Baptism." (*T. D.* 120).

The vehement ardor of St. Louis' love, of which Pope Pius XII spoke, found its flaming expression in *consecration.* No gesture of piety this, but a sublime oblation of the will, freely and joyously conforming it utterly to the Divine.

Conformity to the Divine Will—this is the highest perfection which man can ever attain. It simply means being conformed to the Divine Mold. Clinging to our own will in anything at all means that union with the Divinity is expected to occur by the mold's changing to fit the base metal poured into it. The result would be distortion and ugliness. But a conformity that holds back nothing at all, not even the disposition of our prayers and disposable merits—this is what the consecration of St. Louis De Montfort, fully lived, achieves.

He did not look upon the will to make this complete sacrifice of self as the ultimate goal, something to be attained only after years of endeavor. Boldly and unhesitatingly he establishes this as the very gateway to the practice of his devotion. True, he prescribes a three-week preparation for the solemn event, a vigil of arms before making the pledge of fealty to the Liege Lord and to the Mistress of All. But as the knight proved his loyalty not so much by the oath of fealty as by his subsequent defense of his lord, so the vassal of the Lord of Lords and His Immaculate Queen will prove his fidelity not so much by the Act of Consecration itself as by his subsequent loyal living of it until death.

St. Louis left to the world a sublime formula for making this initial consecration. He entitled it: *"Consecration to Jesus Christ, the Incarnate Wisdom, through the Blessed Virgin Mary."* The first part of the prayer is addressed to Jesus, and the remainder, including the actual words of the oblation, to Mary. Our Lady is the proximate and immediate object of devotion, but the ultimate and final one is Jesus. The Saint esteemed consecration to Mary as the surest and best way of being truly consecrated to her Divine Son.

THE ACT OF CONSECRATION

This is the formula whose making and living has opened the heavens for so many favored souls:

"O Eternal and Incarnate Wisdom! O sweetest and most adorable Jesus! True God and true man, only Son of the Eternal Father, and of Mary, always virgin! I adore Thee profoundly in the bosom and splendors of Thy Father during eternity; and I adore Thee also in the virginal bosom of Mary, Thy most worthy Mother, in the time of Thine Incarnation.

"I give Thee thanks for that Thou hast annihilated Thyself, taking the form of a slave in order to rescue me from the cruel slavery of the devil. I praise and glorify Thee for that Thou hast been pleased to submit Thyself to Mary, Thy holy Mother, in all things, in order to make me Thy faithful slave through her. But, alas! Ungrateful and faithless as I have been, I have

not kept the promises which I made so solemnly to Thee in my Baptism; I have not fulfilled my obligations; I do not deserve to be called Thy child, nor yet Thy slave; and as there is nothing in me which does not merit Thine anger and Thy repulse, I dare not come by myself before Thy most holy and august Majesty. It is on this account that I have recourse to the intercession of Thy most holy Mother, whom Thou hast given me for a mediatrix with Thee. It is through her that I hope to obtain of Thee contrition, the pardon of my sins, and the acquisition and preservation of wisdom.

"Hail, then, O Immaculate Mary, living tabernacle of the Divinity, where the Eternal Wisdom willed to be hidden and to be adored by angels and by men! Hail, O Queen of Heaven and earth, to whose empire everything is subject which is under God. Hail, O sure Refuge of Sinners, whose mercy fails no one. Hear the desires which I have of the Divine Wisdom; and for that end receive the vows and offerings which in my lowliness I present to thee.

"I, N., a faithless sinner, renew and ratify today in thy hands the vows of my Baptism; I renounce forever Satan, his pomps and works; and I give myself entirely to Jesus Christ, the Incarnate Wisdom, to carry my cross after Him all the days of my life, and to be more faithful to Him than I have ever been before.

"In the presence of all the heavenly court I choose thee this day for my Mother and Mistress. I deliver and consecrate to thee, as thy slave, my body and soul, my goods, both interior and exterior, and even the value of all my good actions, past, present and future; leaving to thee the entire and full right of disposing of me, and all that belongs to me, without exception, according to thy good pleasure, for the greater glory of God, in time and in eternity.

"Receive, O benignant Virgin, this little offering of my slavery, in honor of, and in union with, that subjection which the Eternal Wisdom deigned to have to thy maternity, in homage to the power which both of you have over this poor sinner, and in thanksgiving for the privileges with which the Holy Trinity has favored thee. I declare that I wish henceforth, as thy true slave, to seek thy honor and to obey thee in all things.

"O admirable Mother, present me to thy dear Son as His eternal slave, so that as He has redeemed me by thee, by thee He may receive me! O Mother of mercy, grant me the grace to obtain the true Wisdom of God; and for that end receive me among those whom thou lovest and teachest, whom thou leadest, nourishest and protectest as thy children and thy slaves.

"O faithful Virgin, make me in all things so perfect a disciple, imitator and slave of the Incarnate Wisdom, Jesus Christ thy Son, that I may attain, by thine intercession and by thine example, to the fullness of His age on earth and of His glory in Heaven. Amen."

Chapter 3

CONSECRATION TO MARY

Like the word *devotion*, the word *consecration* is also used strictly and loosely. In the latter sense, it means a more or less comprehensive resolve to be united to Mary and work with her and through her to obtain the greater honor and glory of God and union with Him. Strictly, and by definition, it means "to set aside something as sacred, for sacred uses." This is precisely what the Act of Consecration of St. Louis effects.

How often in prayer we use the phrase: "I consecrate myself," and afterwards cannot explain very clearly just what we have done, or how we differ from what we were before. But the one who has made this Act knows definitely what he has done and the new order into which he has introduced himself. He will say:

"I am now a willing and happy slave of love to my Queen Mother and to my Eternal King. I do not bow my head in shame at this slavery, for I serve my Queen, I wear her livery, her mantle encompasses me. She now holds title to me, by my own will, and to all my goods temporal and spiritual, internal and external. She does not necessarily deprive me of the use of any or all of them, but nothing belongs to me any more, and my use of them depends upon her good pleasure. Her love is my reward, and it is all-sufficient. To her I have surrendered any dominion I might otherwise have over all my merits, past, present and future, insofar as I am able to do so. I have given to her all the value of my prayers of petition, and all my acts of satisfaction and atonement. But I know that my Queen is immeasurably more generous than I will ever be, and I have no fear that I or anyone else will ever suffer for what I have done by my consecration. All space cannot contain the ocean of love that is Mary, and though I should walk in the valley of the shadow of death, I will not fear, for Mary is with me.

"Loving her and serving her, I love and serve my King, for this is His will. She will invest me and adorn me, and some blessed day I shall enter into their unveiled presence, never to be parted from them, throughout all ages of ages."

SCOPE OF THE OBLATION

What do we surrender to Mary for her use and possession?

All that we *can* and *may*.

ALL THAT WE CAN:

The merits of every good work are divided into three parts: the one that we cannot give away, and is our inalienable possession; the one that we must give away, for we are members of the Mystical Body, and as such labor not for ourselves alone, but for the whole Body, and the one that it is up to us to keep or give away. It is this last we surrender, without attaching any strings to our offer.

ALL THAT WE MAY:

Sometimes by virtue of our state of life we are bound to apply some of the fruits of our actions for a specific purpose. The priesthood cannot reject the request of the laity to offer the Holy Sacrifice for their specific intentions.

Now it must be remembered that the value of the

Mass is infinite, and so can be offered for a number of intentions at the same time. It must be remembered that the priest derives a very special benefit of the Mass, so do the acolytes, and also those who attend, and of course, those for whom it is offered. All that belongs to him as a result of the Holy Sacrifice the priest is free to surrender to Mary, but not the rest. Nor is the priest inhibited by the Act of Consecration from accepting Mass intentions; it is his duty to be at the disposal of the faithful to offer sacrifice for them.

The pastor of a parish is required by the Church to offer Mass on Sundays and some other days for his people. He is not free to dispose of the fruits that belong to his people, only those which belong to him.

The religious who are required by rule or obedience to offer prayers for some particular intention are not free to give these away, even to Mary, nor does she expect it. She is far more concerned with our obligations than we are ourselves, and would not accept them for other purposes. Of course all petitions must go through her to the Throne of God, and our wills should concur in sending these petitions through her.

Indeed, so much is Mary interested in our obligations, that when we surrender to her all that we are free to give, she will take care of these demands first, and far better than ever we would do by ourselves. For she is not swayed by our personal and mundane likes and dislikes. Do we not pray hardest for the things in which we are interested personally, and often pay but little heed to the things that God and Mary are interested in—the extension of His Kingdom, the spiritual welfare of people we do not know or for whom we have an aversion, for the Pope and the leaders of the Church of Christ, for the sick, the dying, the discouraged, the tempted, and other things too numerous to mention?

The one who puts all into the hands of Mary knows that all his obligations will be taken care of to the extent of the means he places in her hands. He can rest assured too, that all his prayers and works will be used for the greater honor and glory of God. When we specify our intentions, they may be good, but we cannot be certain that they are the ones that God prefers. But when we surrender all into the hands of Mary, we know for certain that they will redound to His greatest honor and glory, because she knows what He prefers and will use them for that purpose.

Like the husband who puts his paycheck into the hands of his wife, a capable and good manager, knows that all bills will be paid promptly, if he gives her enough money with which to pay them, and that the best possible use will be made of the remaining money; so we can be absolutely certain and content that when we place everything in Mary's hands, she will do the same for us. All we have to do is to give her enough.

NO ONE THE LOSER

Making this offering will never occasion loss on our part nor on the part of anyone else.

"If you then being evil, know how to give good gifts to your children," said Our Lord, *"how much more will your Father, who is in heaven, give good things to them that ask him?"* (Matt. 7:11). And we might add, for it is true, *"...and Mary!"*

All the generosity imaginable in us earthbound mortals is no more than a spark of the generosity of God, who is Generosity and Love, and of the generosity of Mary, His faithful image.

No generous person will ever wish to be outdone in generosity. The Heavenly Father will never allow it to happen to Him, neither will Mary. Generous giving will meet with generous return. Unlimited giving will meet with undreamed of returns. The more we give, the more we shall get back. This is the way of God, and of Mary, His beloved spouse.

But what about spiritual bouquets, and prayers that others request us to say for them? Can we continue to promise these things if we make the Act of Consecration?

Indeed we can. But how is this possible, if we have surrendered title to all that we can give away?

Let us suppose that a little child has saved up his money to buy Christmas presents, a sum insignificant to his parents, but vast to him. But when the time comes to buy, his love for his mother proves so great that he spends all his money on a present for her, and has nothing left for the others. The day comes to present the gift to her, and she exclaims: "But my dear, you have spent all your money on me; you have nothing left for anyone else!" and he answers: "I know, but I love you so much I couldn't help it." If that mother has ample means, will she allow his friends to go without gifts? Will she not herself be generous to them, singing in her heart because of her child's love?

Mary has the infinite Treasury at her command. When we give her our all, is there nothing left to give to others? Of course we cannot demand her to do so, but he who knows the Heart of Mary knows what she will do!

But what if we have already deeded all our merits to the Poor Souls in the Heroic Act of Charity? Are we not forever enjoined from making the Act of Consecration, having nothing further to give away?

No, we are not.

No one is impeded from making a more perfect act by reason of a less perfect one previously made. The

Act of Consecration to the Blessed Virgin Mary is more perfect than the Heroic Act of Charity, magnificent and sublime as that unquestionably is.

Sanctity is proportioned to our conformity to the will of God. There is greater conformity to God's will in the Act of Consecration than in the Heroic Act. The latter designates the recipient; there is a string attached to the gift. The former leaves God utterly unfettered; conformity of will is complete.

Can we be absolutely sure that God would not prefer to use our good works, at least sometimes, to lead souls to Him who are still in this life, and who would otherwise be lost? What brings more glory to Him: to place additional souls before the Throne forever, souls who would never get there otherwise, or to shorten the exile of those who are already His?

But if we have made the Heroic Act, and now make the Act of Consecration, will not the Poor Souls be the losers? Not at all.

The supreme love, trust and confidence evoked in making and living the Consecration will bring a new wealth of graces that would never have been ours had we not made the Act. But once we have made it, we may rely on Our Lady to pay off the mortgage on our good works, and to give to the Poor Souls all that they otherwise would have been entitled to, and still have a lot left over, for them and for the other intentions close and dear to her Immaculate Heart.

CHILDREN
AND THE ACT OF CONSECRATION

Some are disturbed by anxious fears when the Consecration is preached to children, fearing that the little ones cannot comprehend sufficiently the implications and sublimity of this Act.

Such fears were entertained for a long time, and indeed up to the recent past (1910) about something immeasurably more sacred than even the Act of Consecration. It had been unheard of for a long time to make it a practice of giving Holy Communion to children of seven years of age. What child, they argued, of those years could comprehend what he was doing when he received the incomparable Sacrament—the Lord of the Universe, the King of Kings, the Infinite Splendor?

But Pius X, the saintly Flaming Fire of love for God, for children and for all mankind, cut through all vain reasoning, and despite all wonder and dismay issued his blessed Encyclical on Frequent Communion, and the little ones thronged to the altar all over the world to receive into their hearts, to embrace, and to be embraced by the Lover of Children. Thereafter the Lord has been allowed to come to them in their tender, formative years to bend the little tree His way, to flood with light and grace, before it may be too late.

Yes, the Holy Father knew that many of these children would later evict their Lord from their hearts by mortal sin. But He also reasoned that if they were so weak as to do that after having been fortified by the Sacrament, what would have happened to them had they not received this strength, in an ever-worsening world? But now early and frequent Communion is so dear to the hearts of the faithful that it will never again be taken from the little ones.

In the revelations vouchsafed to Lucy of Fatima, of which more will be said later (Chapter V), Heaven called for the consecration of the world to the Immaculate Heart.

"The world" means the children, too.

When St. Louis De Montfort wrote over two hundred years ago, he said that this devotion he was preaching was a secret, and was not to be told to anyone except those whose lives proved they would make the most of it. But the pronouncement of Heaven, the words that invited all the world, seemingly have rent the veil of the secret as was rent the veil of the Temple that separated the Holy Place from the Holy of Holies. That torn veil long ago bespoke the fact that the Law of Fear had ended, and the Law of Love had begun. Men, all men, were thereafter to approach the Lord their God with joyous affection, now shown forth in all His Love as Our Father. The invitation to universal consecration has rent the veil of the "Secret of Mary," and every man, every woman and every child is called to come forthwith to the embrace of Mary and to be sheltered under her mantle. Who will doubt that the Age of Mary has begun?

AUTHORITIES

The devotion of St. Louis De Montfort is still unknown to the vast majority of men, but it is not due to the lack of warm praise and affection from the highest authorities in the Church.

Pope Leo XIII made the Act of Consecration and blessed the Confraternity of Mary Queen of All Hearts, the association of those who practice this devotion.

Pope Pius X granted the Apostolic Benediction to all who would read *True Devotion to the Blessed Virgin Mary*, and raised the Confraternity to the dignity of an Archconfraternity.

Benedict XV declared the book to be "of such high authority and unction." (Letter to the Superior General of the Company of Mary).

Pope Pius XI replied to Cardinal Mercier, who had spoken to him of this devotion: "Not only do I know it, but I have practiced it from my youth." (*T. D.*— Introduction).

Pope Pius XII canonized St. Louis and eulogized his writings.

Cardinal O'Connell, while Spiritual Director of the North American College in Rome, taught it and recommended it to his seminarians.

Cardinal Stritch made the Act of Consecration publicly when he erected the Confraternity of Mary Queen of All Hearts in his Archdiocese at St. Francis Xavier Church, Chicago, on October 17, 1946.

Father Faber spoke in 1862 the conviction and hopes of the now ever more rapidly increasing number of Mary's devoted children, old and young, cleric and lay.

"Jesus is obscured because Mary is kept in the background...God is pressing for a wider, a stronger, quite another devotion to His Blessed Mother...Oh, if Mary were but known, there would be no coldness to Jesus then! Oh, if Mary were but known, how much more wonderful would be our faith, and how different would our Communions be! Oh, if Mary were but known, how much happier, how much holier, how much less worldly should we be, and how much more should we be living images of our sole Lord and Saviour, her dearest and most blessed Son!...

"May the Holy Ghost, the Divine Zealot of Jesus and Mary, deign to give a new blessing to this work, and may He please to console us quickly with the speedy coming of the great age of the Church which is to be the Age of Mary!" (*T. D.*—Preface).

Chapter 4

LIVING THE CONSECRATION

By making the Act of Consecration, Mary's loyal child takes upon himself the slavery that bears no stigma and enters into the inner circle of her court. Once there, it is not enough to rest and be served. It is time to work and to serve as never before. Thereafter he will do everything she desires, everything that she has made known that there is to do. Mary has so often called men to say the Rosary; that her devoted page will surely do. Atonement and penance—her request at Lourdes, her demand at Fatima—her courtier in this will try to anticipate the wishes of his Queen and give her more than she seeks, with her loving smile his greatest reward. The Scapular, the Miraculous Medal, anything certain and approved, he will make his own, for all his thoughts are for his Queen.

St. Louis further definitizes the mode of procedure for the lover of Mary. He will act *with* her, and *in* her, and *through* her, and *for* her. (*S. M.* 43.).

WITH MARY

He will align himself completely with her will. He will be the unresisting implement in her hand for the accomplishment of the Divine Will that no one else knows so well as she, the brush in the hand of Mary the painter, the chisel in the hand of Mary the sculptor.

Complete conformity to the will of God—that is perfect sanctity.

Nature affords no more beautiful picture of the calm and peace that is man's heritage than a quiet, lonely, pine-fringed lake at sunset. During the day there may have been breezes that stirred the waters, but as evening comes on, the waters begin to still, and long, vague reflections to appear, until at sunset, the wind having died down and the waters stilled, they present a perfect picture below of all that is above.

The soul tossed by anxiety and care of the earth mirrors but poorly the glory of God, but as personal desires lessen, the reflection of Heaven in the soul begins to appear, until at last, the desires all stilled, God is perfectly mirrored, as far as He can be, in the image He has made.

Everyone made by God who reverts to this calm and beautiful reflection of the infinitely beautiful Creator has performed a sublime act of reparation, an act of repairing the nature deformed by sin, and restoring it in one at least, to its pristine beauty.

To make ourselves decrease, that He may increase, and to do this with the aid of Mary, and to help her achieve the same goal in others—this it is to live *with* Mary.

IN MARY

We have to get along in life with our own eyes, our own ears, our own tongue, our own mind and understanding. If we could borrow these from great men, as one draws books from a library, what wonders could we not perform!

Our material senses we cannot borrow, but spiritual ones we can, by effort and by grace. Grace gives us something of the vision of the eyes of Mary, if we want it, the hearing of her ears, the understanding of her mind, the love of her heart. It is up to us to work along with the gift, to develop it to the full. If we really desire it, we shall ever increase in the power of seeing things as she sees them, looking at the things she would look at, scorning the things she scorns; listening to the things she likes to hear, shutting our ears to the rest, judging as she judges, and loving more and more with the love with which she loves. This it is to live *in* Mary.

"Ask, and it shall be given you; seek and you shall find; knock and it shall be opened unto you." (Matt. 7:7).

THROUGH MARY

Does a man enter the home of a friend through the window or through an opened door? Does he climb over a wall, or go through an opened gate?

Mary is the Gate of Heaven. Through her the Lord of Heaven came to us; through her He wishes us to return to Him.

In some things we must go through Mary, whether we will it or not. It is true we can speak to God directly. But He will do nothing unless she asks for us. "No prayer will receive an answer before the Divine Throne unless placed there by the Queen of Heaven herself." *(R. R.).* It did not have to be that way, but it is that way because that is the will of God.

What about prayers of love and praise and thanksgiving? Must they go through her too, as must prayers of petition?

Must they? The question rather should be: "Can it be that the peerless Queen herself will speak for me? Will she take my rude, uncouth efforts and present them before His Majesty in a way suited to His magnificence and glory?"

If we had to write a letter to the Holy Father in Latin, what would the majority of us do? If we had a friend who was an authority on classical Latin, would we give him the idea, and ask him to express it for us as he would know best how to do, or would we just get a Latin grammar and try to figure out for ourselves what to write?

We may be brilliant in earthly science and accomplishments, but what do we know of the ways of the Heavenly Court and the Heart of God? *"For your thoughts are not my Thoughts, nor your ways my ways."* (*Is.* 55:8). He has reminded us. *"As the heavens are exalted above the earth, so are my ways exalted above your ways, and my thoughts above your thoughts."* (*Is.* 55:9).

But Mary knows His ways: she is His daughter, His Mother, His spouse. She is the Queen of Heaven. What a privilege that she will take our clumsy efforts and make them worthy to be spoken to the Lord of Hosts!

So with all our good works—the Queen enhances and beautifies them before she presents them to the King. We are like children. How many a little boy treasures strange odds and ends, which to his elders are so much trash, and would be no suitable present at all! How many a little girl loves devotedly a ragged and nondescript doll that would never belong in the cradle of a prince! If she parted with her treasure to give it to him, it would be a great act of love indeed, but how much better it would be if someone would fix it all up for her like new before it was presented!

That is just what Our Lady does with all the prayers and good works that we send to the Lord our God through her. She embellishes them from the treasury of her Son's merits, all of which are at her command through her intercession. "To Mary, His faithful spouse, God the Holy Ghost has communicated His unspeakable gifts; and He has chosen her to be the dispenser of all He possesses, in such sort that she distributes to whom she wills, as much as she wills, as she wills and when she wills, all His gifts and graces." (*T. D.* 25). "She will communicate herself to us with her merits and virtues; she will place our presents on the golden plate of her charity; she will clothe us, as Rebecca clothed Jacob, with the beautiful garments of her elder and only Son, Jesus Christ—that is, His merits, which she has at her disposal..." (*S. M.* 38).

This claim of St. Louis is so stupendous, so little known, so little preached, so breathtaking in its beauty, that we shall let the Saint speak of it in his own words, words which in the process of his canonization, were adjudged to be free from error:

"As by this practice we give to Our Lord, by His Mother's hands, all our good works, that good Mother purifies them, embellishes them and makes them acceptable to her Son.

"She purifies them of all the stain of self-love, and of that imperceptible attachment to created things which slips unnoticed into our best actions. As soon as they are in her most pure and fruitful hands, those same hands which have never been sullied or idle, and which purify whatever they touch, take away from the present which we make her all that was spoiled or imperfect about it.

"She embellishes our works, adorning them with her own merits and virtues. It is as if a peasant, wishing to gain the friendship and benevolence of the king, went to the queen and presented her with a fruit which was his whole revenue, in order that she might present it to the king. The queen, having accepted the poor little offering from the peasant, would place the fruit on a large and beautiful dish of gold, and so, on the peasant's behalf, would present it to the king. Then the fruit, however unworthy in itself to be a king's present, would become worthy of his majesty, because of the dish of gold on which it rested and the person who presented it." (*T. D.* 146-7).

He looks upon the story of Jacob's obtaining his father's blessing through the activity of his mother Rebecca as a figure of the Blessed Mother's action towards her consecrated child:

"This good mother, having received the perfect offering which we make to her of ourselves and our merits and satisfactions, by the devotion I am describing, strips us of our old garments; she makes us her own and so makes us worthy to appear before our Heavenly Father. (1) She clothes us in clean, new precious and perfumed garments of Esau the elder—this is, of Jesus Christ her Son—which she keeps in her house—that is, which she has in her own power inasmuch as she is the treasurer and universal dispenser of the merits and virtues of her Son, which she gives and communicates to whom she wills, when she wills, as she wills, and in such quantity as she wills, as we have seen before. (2) She covers the neck and the hands of her servants with the skins of the kids she has killed; that is to say, she adorns them with the merits and value of their own actions. She kills and mortifies, it is true, all that is impure and imperfect in them, but she neither loses nor dissipates one atom of the good that grace has done there. On the contrary, she preserves and augments it, to make it the ornament and the strength of their neck and their hands; that is to say, to fortify them and help them carry the yoke of the Lord which is worn upon the neck, and to work great things for the glory of God and the salvation of their poor brethren. (3) She bestows a new perfume and a new grace upon their garments and adornments, in communicating to them her own garments, that is, merits and virtues which she bequeathed to them by her testament when she died; as said a holy religious of the last century, who died in the odor of sanctity, and learned this by revelation. Thus all her domestics, faithful servants and slaves, are doubly clad in the garments of her Son and in her own:

'All her domestics are clothed in double clothing.' (Prov.
31:21)." (*T. D.* 207).

Care must be taken, of course, not to confuse the
doctrine of the Saint with the false teachings of those
who say that good works are not important or necessary and that faith alone sufficing, the merits of Christ
as a mantle cover even mortal sins, and make a person
worthy, without repentance, to enter Heaven. St. Louis
presupposes of course, that the consecrated child of
Mary is in the state of grace and capable of producing
meritorious works. It is these works, already holy, that
she still further sanctifies and embellishes.

What an inestimable privilege and blessing! Who
can boast that his prayers and good works are perfect?
No self-seeking therein, no self-satisfaction, no hidden
motives not clear to him but clear to God? If we constantly see people who have faults they never suspect,
must we not be apprehensive that the same may be
true of us, especially in the eyes of God?

But when we humbly recognize all these possibili-
ties, and ask Our Lady to make our poor gifts more
presentable, she will graciously give them her loving
care, adorning them with her own virtues and merits
and those of her Divine Son, and they will emerge from
her hands free of blemish and worthy to be placed before the King.

Do we feel ourselves as worthy as Mary to appear
before the splendor of His Sanctity and Majesty? Then
what should ever hold us back from going to God
through her, always and in everything?

FOR MARY

Does working for Mary imply acting for her rather
than for the Lord, pleasing her and ignoring Him? God
forbid!

Mary's will is completely united to the will of God. We cannot please her without pleasing Him; we cannot please Him without pleasing her.

The ultimate and final reason for doing all that we do must be to please God, and to unite ourselves to Him. Vast and incomprehensible as is her dignity, the glory of the All is infinitely greater.

God is and must be the principal end of all our actions. Mary is secondary, but inseparably connected.

"And thou shalt love the Lord thy God with thy whole heart, and with thy whole soul, and with thy whole mind. This is the greatest and the first commandment.

"And the second is like to this: Thou shalt love thy neighbor as thyself." (Matt. 22:37-39).

These are two Commandments, yet in a sense they are one. The first obliges us to love God for His own sake. The second commands us to love our neighbor. But why? On account of his intrinsic worth, totally unrelated to God? Not at all. All that is lovable in man is so simply because it is a reflection of the Divine Excellence. In one case it is God we love in Himself; in the second it is really God we love too, but in His image.

Sometimes it is hard for us to realize that certain individuals are made to the image and likeness of God, so hidden is that likeness under a fearful mask of depravity and corruption. But there is no excuse for our not loving with all the power of our soul, His Image as revealed in Our Lady. Always excepting the human nature of her Son, hypostatically united to the Divinity, she is the most glorious masterpiece that has ever proceeded from the hand of God. She is the Mirror of Justice that reflects with dazzling brilliance the Divine Splendor. If we love God we must love Mary, love her as we love no one below her, for her likeness to

Him will forever exceed our powers of comprehension. If we love Mary, we must love God, for everything in her that is lovable, as is the case with all the rest of us, is so simply because it reflects the splendor of the Lord, only she is ineffably more perfect a mirror than we are.

It is difficult indeed to love God in His image when that likeness is befouled and besmirched, dim and almost unrecognizable.

By our obedience in doing our best, we perform a great act of love for God. But we simply cannot love one who mirrors only a few of His perfections, and then but poorly, as much as we can one who reflects His glories in uncounted number, and to unspeakable perfection. We cannot love what is not there. By loving Mary as we should love her, we love God in His image as far as it is possible for us to do so.

To do all that we do for God and for Mary, in other words, for Him in Himself and in His image—that is the perfect observance of the First and the Second Great Commandments, and they comprise all the Law and all the Prophets.

Chapter 5

CONSECRATION AND FATIMA

The story of the apparitions at Fatima is too well known now to need detailed repetition here. The whole Catholic world has heard how Our Lady appeared on May 13, 1917 to three Portuguese children, Lucy, Jacinta and Francis, and then again once each month until the following October, when she sealed her testimony with the great miracle of the sun. Through the years, further revelations were made by Our Lord and Our Lady to Lucy, all of which are summed up in the title: "The Message of Fatima."

In the briefest possible words, the Message of Fatima stressed three things:

ROSARY
REPARATION
CONSECRATION

These were not simple requests; the Message was marked by ominous urgency.

The call to the Rosary was not new. She had already spoken at Lourdes of the need of that great prayer. Neither was the call to Reparation. That too she had stressed at the same time. Morever, in the preceding century Jesus had likewise made known the need of atonement, in the revelations of His Sacred Heart.

What was new was the call to devotion to the Immaculate Heart of Mary and the consecration to that Immaculate Heart. It was made known that it was the will (not the desire, nor request, nor hope, but the *will*) of the Heavenly Father that all the world be consecrated to her Immaculate Heart.

Let us review the evidence for this statement, which has been challenged by some.

We quote from the *Crusade of Fatima* by Fr. John De Marchi (Kenedy, 1948, page 47 *sq.*).

"Our Lady explained: You have seen Hell—where the souls of poor sinners go. To save them God wants to establish throughout the world the devotion to my Immaculate Heart.

"If people will do what I tell you, many souls will be saved, and there will be peace. The war is going to end.

"But if they do not stop offending God, another and worse war will break out in the reign of Pius XI. When you see a night illumined by an unknown light, know that it is the great sign that God gives you that He is going to punish the world for its crimes by means of war, hunger, persecution of the Church and of the Holy Father.

"To prevent this, I shall come to ask for the consecration of Russia to my Immaculate Heart and the Communion of Reparation on the First Saturdays.

"If they heed my requests, Russia will be converted and there will be peace. If not, she shall spread her errors throughout the world, promoting wars and persecutions of the Church; the good will be martyred, the Holy Father will have much to suffer, various nations will be annihilated; in the end, my Immaculate Heart will triumph. The Holy Father will consecrate Russia to me, which will be converted, and some time of peace will be given to the world...

"Do not tell this to anyone. To Francis, yes, you may tell it." (*C. F.* p. 47).

In 1927, Lucy received permission to tell of this vision of Hell and the urgent need for devotion to the
Immaculate Heart of Mary. (*C. F.* p. 155).

It was in 1927, while she was praying in the convent
chapel at Tuy, Spain, where she was then stationed, that
she received permission from Heaven to reveal the first
two parts of the secret, the vision of Hell and the urgent
need for devotion to the Immaculate Heart of Mary.

"Two years later, in 1929, Our Lady again appeared
to Lucy while she was praying in the chapel at Tuy.
This was the time chosen by our Lady to fulfill her
previous request: 'I shall come to ask the consecration
of Russia to my Immaculate Heart: . . . If they heed my
request, Russia will be converted, and there will be
peace.' Our Lady explained that this consecration should
be made by the Holy Father in unison with all the
Bishops of the world." (*C. F.* 155).

But nothing was done for many years. Then in 1940,
Lucy wrote to the Bishop of Leiria:

"In 1940, Lucy wrote again to the Bishop of Leiria
expressing her regret that the consecration had not yet
been made. 'Would that the world knew the hour of
grace that is being given it and would do penance.'
Then she wrote directly to Pope Pius XII at the command of her spiritual directors, telling him the *exact
request* of Our Lady. Lucy asked for *the consecration
of the world to Mary's Immaculate Heart with a special mention of Russia.*

"The Pope deliberated long and prayerfully upon this
request of Mary. In 1942, the Clergy and people of
Portugal celebrated the silver anniversary of the apparitions of Fatima. On the last day of October of the
same year, the Bishops of the country gathered at the
shrine to join with the Holy Father in fulfilling the
request of Our Lady. The Pope at that time consecrated

the Church and the world to her Immaculate Heart, including the people of Russia by these words:

"'Give peace to the peoples separated from us by error or by schism and especially to the one who professes such singular devotion to thee and in whose homes an honored place was ever accorded thy venerable icon (today often kept hidden to await better days); bring them back to the one fold of Christ under the one true Shepherd...' Six weeks later, on the feast of the Immaculate Conception, in the presence of 40,000 people, the Holy Father repeated this consecration at St. Peter's in Rome. This consecration was a decisive event in the history of the world; it marks the beginning of a new era, the Age of Mary.

"The following spring, our Blessed Lord appeared to Lucia to express the joy of His Heart over this consecration. Lucia tells about it in a letter to the Bishop of Gurza, her spiritual director.

"'Your Excellency,' Lucia wrote, 'The good Lord has already shown me His pleasure in the act of the Holy Father and the various Bishops, although incomplete according to His desire...'

"Our Lord said that the act of the Holy Father is incomplete, *But it cannot be completed until every individual, every home, every diocese and every country consecrates itself, after the example of the Holy Father to the Immaculate Heart.* For as the Bishop of Leiria wrote: 'At the request of the Bishops of Portugal and of Sr. Lucia herself, the Holy Father, in the course of his famous message to Portugal at the close of the Fatima Jubilee on October 31, 1942, made the consecration of the world to the Immaculate Heart of Mary, *a consecration we must all repeat officially and personally.*'"(C. F. 157 sq.).

In May, 1948, Pope Pius XII issued an encyclical to

the whole world, calling upon every family and every diocese to concur in this consecration.

Consecration and Reparation are closely allied. The reparation which the Lord now seeks is the sacrifice of self necessary to obtain union with Him, the sacrifice involved in the perfect observance of the duties of our state of life. Consecration to the Immaculate Heart is union with Mary, the most efficient and admirable means for finding Jesus, loving Him, doing His will to perfection, and of obtaining with Him eternal union.

"This is the penance which the good Lord now asks: the sacrifice that every person has to impose upon himself is to lead a life of justice in the observance of His Law. He requires that this way be made known to souls. For many, thinking that the word penance means great austerities and not feeling in themselves the strength or generosity for these, lose heart and rest in a life of lukewarmness and sin.

"Last Thursday, at midnight, while I was in chapel with my superiors' permission, Our Lord said to me: 'The sacrifice required of every person is the fulfillment of his duties in life and the observance of My Law. This is the penance I now seek and require.'" (*C. F.* p. 159).

What is called for is *a return to the right order of living*, to the order that would have existed had there been no Fall of our first parents, no Original Sin, no distortion of nature. The Fall sent the magnificent edifice of man's nature, and the world that was to serve him, crashing into ruins; Reparation is *repairing* the damage.

When a man loves the Lord with his whole heart and with his whole soul and with his whole mind and with all his strength, and his neighbor as himself for the love of God—then he has done the repairing that

God seeks, and in that one soul at least Reparation has been accomplished.

Nature before the Fall was like a beautiful city, with wide shaded streets, beautiful parks and stately mansions. After the catastrophe it is like that same city following a devastating air raid—bombed out, with its streets heaps of rubble, its parks gaunt, dead wastes, its lovely homes blackened and gutted. After the scourge has passed, it is up to the citizen to rebuild, and to remove the scars of war. Materials are available for the asking, but application must be made. The damage will not be fully repaired while one eyesore remains. If the owner will do nothing, it is up to the other citizens to see to it that he is aroused to a sense of responsibility, or to help him if he has been stricken down.

God wants all nature repaired, and put into the same order it was before the great disaster. Some will not do anything at all. Some must be awakened to their duty; others must be helped. Our responsibility for reparation does not end in ourselves. We are all one family under God. True reparation requires that the world come to believe this again, and to *act its belief*.

A homely example may serve to emphasize the need of reparation:

A father comes home at night after a trying day at the office. He just wants to sit down and relax and read his paper. The children begin to whine and fight. Their mother warns them that their father is in no mood to tolerate any annoyance. They do not listen, but begin to chase each other around the house, tripping over their father's feet. At last he gives them a slap, but it does no good. Their mother warns them again, yet they run around all the faster, tumbling over tables and chairs, knocking over lamps and vases. Then their father gives them a thorough trouncing, but scarcely has he sat down when they start up again, worse than before, throwing things and smashing windows.

What will a strong, determined, able-bodied father do then?

Our Lady appeared at Lourdes and said it was high time to stop this endless offending of God, and to get busy at once to put everything back in order and act like well-bred, considerate children. Her warning was disregarded; the Commandments were broken as always, and worse. The Eternal Father waited a long time, but in 1914 came the first World War, which was thought at the time to be a dreadful scourge, but was only a slap in view of what happened later. In 1917 she warned her children again, and told them with all possible urgency that they must behave, or else. Again she was ignored, and so came World War II and the pernicious errors that bereft civilization of its senses, and spawned the most ghastly horrors the world has ever known. And still man sins. God is still ignored; His punishments up to now have not brought the modern world one bit closer to Him. Nature is still substituted for the Creator, man still rejoices in the dim light of the human intellect and ignores the Light Divine, still they curse and perjure, profane the Sabbath, reject the principle of authority, trample on human rights, prostitute marriage, cheat, connive and steal, smear and slander.

The Lord of Might and Justice, of Sanctity and Truth—what is He supposed to do? Does anything in Revelation indicate that this merry-go-round of service and disservice, fidelity and infidelity is to go on forever?

He is the God of patience beyond all patience, love beyond all love, but God is not mocked. The wheat and the tares will grow together until the harvest, but the Harvest will come, the tares will be burned, the wheat gathered into His barns.

God cannot again grant peace in our time unless first there is a profound moral revolution. We have behind us the shame of the decade which has come to be known as the Terrible Twenties, the era of hip flasks and flaming youth, when pleasure was god. And now, with the tremendous advances in science, the extraordinary achievements that come crowding and tumbling out of the laboratories, all designed to make this earthly life more completely satisfying, what would happen if God gave peace, and let unregenerated man rush back to his comfortable and enticing world? Can a sensible father give an irresponsible, bibulous adolescent an automobile?

A sensible father cannot grant all his children's whims, much as he would like to, because he knows they would become spoiled. There is nothing the Heavenly Father would like better than to make us happy, but unless we are morally strong we cannot stand much of the heady wine of temporal prosperity. Especially now, when man has gotten out of hand altogether, is it necessary for Him to use drastic measures. They must change or be lost. They have not listened to Him yet, and if they will not, they leave Him no alternative but to use sterner measures still.

Yes, reparation is the desperate need of our times, and the Divine call to offer it must be obeyed by every man, every woman and every child without delay. Perhaps "it is later than you think."

The demand for reparation should not frighten anyone, nor make him feel he is called to a repugnant, miserable task. Reparation is the fruit of love. Is love bitter and repellent? Is it hard to love what is good and beautiful? Should it be hard to love the All-Good, the All-Beautiful? Should it be hard to welcome the return of the right order, good and beautiful too? If we are conscious that we have behaved shamefully to a true friend, whose love has not been changed by our miserable disloyalty and cheap ingratitude, is it hard to go beyond our ordinary signs of friendship to convince him that we are truly sorry and wish to make amends.

That is all that God looks for, and we shall do that eagerly as soon as we love the Lord our God with all our heart and soul.

The decree of the Eternal Father that all the world be consecrated to the Immaculate Heart of Mary is simply the full flowering of the Divine Plan of reparation, of the rebuilding into a strong and perpetual order of peace and joy the nature of the children of men.

The exact formula for the consecration was not revealed, nor were all of its essential components specifically stated. But the one who makes and lives the Act of Consecration of St. Louis De Montfort will be sure to obey the Divine injunction, for this act is all-embracing.

Love is giving; love is proved by sacrifice. When we give all, we love best. When we become a royal servant of Mary by giving her everything we have to give away, and really mean what we say and abide by our word, then love can do no more, except from then on to work unceasingly for the Queen, obeying her every wish and command, until at last with her faithful children all around her, never to be parted again, the Queen of Heaven and Earth is crowned Queen of the New Creation.

Consecration and the living of that consecration, the doing of everything Her Majesty wishes with alacrity and joy, the anticipating of her wishes, the seeking to surprise her, if that were possible, by trying to give more, the ceaseless endeavor to be perfectly united to her in thought and will, character, virtue and love, and through her, to her glorious Divine Son—this is the full-blown rose of Reparation.

Reparation animated by Consecration, with the Rosary, giving the inspiration, the strength and the love for both, and for all they imply—this is the Message of Fatima.

DUTY OF THE INDIVIDUAL

Salvation is an affair of each individual. So is the reparation now sought and demanded; so is the consecration.

We may draw down from Heaven by prayer and good works graces for others which will touch hearts of flint, but each must ultimately make his own decision to love God above all things. The final choice of salvation or damnation rests with the individual. No one can be saved against his will. He must personally concur with the graces won for him by the rest of the Mystical Body.

The reparation that God seeks is the aligning of all wills with His, the union of man with God. This is the primeval order. To satisfy the Divine will completely, each and every human will must concur in this restoration. No one can straighten a bent nature against its will. It must yield by a personal fiat to all that is being done for it. No one can assume that the penances of Trappists and Poor Clares, and the good works of good people everywhere, are going to take the place of his personal acquiescence and submission to the sweet yoke of God, so that he can ride into Heaven on their merits. In the ultimate analysis, it is the individual who must say: "I do."

So too is the Consecration an affair of the individual will. Both words are important: "individual" and "will."

It is an act of the *will* that is required, not a play of emotions. Some say acts of consecration, but only their feelings are aroused, not their will. This is like painting a house with whitewash; it looks all right until the winds and the rains and the storms come.

The consecration must be an act of the *individual*, for to mean anything, it must ultimately be an act of the individual will, and only the individual can command his own will.

The Holy Father gave a shining example to the world on December 8, 1942, by consecrating it to the Immaculate Heart of Mary. But He did not intend this to supply the need for personal concurrence in his action.

The Pope made up the train, the swift express that will bear us to the Heart of God. We must board it of our own free will. He set up the ladder to Heaven, and we must climb. He built the house, and we must live in it.

His Eminence, Samuel Cardinal Stritch, likewise gave resplendent example to his Archdiocese of Chicago and to all good people everywhere, when he knelt before the altar of St. Francis Xavier Church, Chicago, on the occasion of the opening of a solemn, perpetual novena to the Immaculate Heart of our Lady of Fatima, recited the Rosary, said prayers of love and praise, and made the sublime Act of Consecration of St. Louis De Montfort. He then issued an invitation to others to do the same by canonically erecting in that parish the Confraternity of Mary Queen of All Hearts, which has for its main object the making and the living of that Act of Consecration. Having established the Confraternity, he personally signed his name in the Register as its first member.

The Vicar of Christ and a Prince of the Church, the one the head of the Church and the other the head of the largest archdiocese, one consecrating the world, the other giving the example of personal concurrence— what more is needed to show men the way to the Heart of Mary and so to the Heart of God?

Chapter 6

THE ARCHCONFRATERNITY OF MARY QUEEN OF ALL HEARTS

Many societies and confraternities exist which sponsor a growing love for the Rosary; the same is true of societies and confraternities for reparation. There is one that has for its main object Consecration, the perfect Consecration and its subsequent living—the Archconfraternity of Mary Queen of All Hearts.

It was first founded in 1899 by Archbishop Duhamel in Ottawa, Canada. Leo XIII blessed the Confraternity and Pius X raised the Confraternity in Rome to the dignity of an Archconfraternity.

Membership in the Confraternity is acquired by entering the applicant's name in the official register.

Membership requirements are simple:

1. *Prior to enrollment the applicant must consecrate himself to the Blessed Virgin Mary, using the Consecration of St. Louis De Montfort.*

2. *The members should live with a Marian spirit— doing all things with Mary, through Mary, in Mary, and for Mary.*

3. *Members should renew the Consecration faithfully and frequently, making a special practice of renewing it every morning at the beginning of each new day. The donation of self can easily be renewed from time to time during the day by repeating*

the short formula: "I am all Thine and all I have is Thine, O most loving Jesus, through Mary, Thy holy Mother." The Consecration can even be renewed by a mere interior act of the mind.

The members also have an obligation to publicize Marian teaching, especially that of St. Louis De Montfort, that all may come to acknowledge and honor the Blessed Virgin as their Mother and Queen.

It is commendable to make a small offering or to do a good work in honor of Our Lady on the day of Consecration.

It is also recommended to wear the medal of Mary, Queen of All Hearts.

"Where two or three are gathered together in My Name, there I am in the midst of them." Those who are devoted to Our Lady should not rest in personal action, but should give their names to the Confraternity, and linked by a common bond of love of God and Mary, present a united force against the spirit of the world, and present a united front for the honor and glory of God and the Immaculate Heart of His Mother.

PRIESTS OF MARY

The priests who join the Confraternity are called Priests of Mary. It is their desire to spread complete love and service to their Queen. Outside of making the most of the opportunities afforded them by their state in life, their membership requirements are the same as for all other members.

Joining the Priests of Mary is something that merits the attention of everyone able to do so. Experience has shown what peace and what power it brings in the exercise of the sacred ministry. In giving their all to her, those "other Christs" simply follow the example of her Divine Son, who gave to her by grace all that was His by nature, as far as it was possible for Him to give. They imitate the example of the Divinity, who made His Spouse the dispenser of all His graces.

His yoke is sweet, and His burden is light, and so is the servitude of Mary, Mediatrix of All Graces, Mother of All Mankind, Queen of Heaven and Earth—full of grace and truth, and light and life, and so it will remain, in time and in eternity.

QUEEN OF ALL HEARTS

Innumerable are the titles that are Mary's by the grace and love of the Eternal Father, and by her faithful and joyous correspondence with every least grace that came down to her from Heaven. God gave her by grace all that He could give her that was His by nature. We could go on and on forever reciting the litany of her titles and praises.

But may we never forget that one title that only man can bestow upon her, that one realm of which only he can crown her Queen. Even the Heavenly Father, by His eternal decree, cannot command in that kingdom, and with longing He waits upon man to crown Him King, and desiring she desires to receive the diadem of Queen of that realm of the hearts of men.

To make the Act of Consecration is to crown her Queen of our Heart, and to join the Confraternity is to help to extend her dominion.

May she rule over earth and sea and the heavens above, over Patriarchs, Prophets, Apostles and Evangelists, Angels and Archangels, Cherubim and Seraphim, but most of all may she reign over the free wills, the hearts of men, the peerless, the lovely, the glorious

Queen of All Hearts!

*"As the vine I have brought forth a pleasant odour:
and my flowers are the fruit of honour and riches. I
am the mother of fair love, and of fear, and of knowledge, and of holy hope. In me is all grace of the way
and of the truth, in me is all hope of life and of virtue.
Come over to me, all ye that desire me, and be filled
with my fruits. For my spirit is sweet above honey,
and my inheritance above honey and the honeycomb.
My memory is unto everlasting generations. They that
eat me, shall yet hunger: and they that drink me, shall
yet thirst. He that hearkeneth to me, shall not be con-
founded: and they that work by me, shall not sin. They
that explain me shall have life everlasting."* (*Ecclus.*
24:23-31).

———

Those who wish to spread knowledge of the De Montfort way or who wish to be enrolled in the Confraternity are invited to address

The Confraternity of
Mary Queen of All Hearts
26 S. Saxon Ave.
Bay Shore, NY 11706

Those enrolling should send their name, address and
date of consecration.

If you have enjoyed this book, consider making your next selection from among the following . . .

Prices subject to change.

Moments Divine—Before Bl. Sacrament *Reuter* 10.00
Saints Who Raised/Dead—400 Resurrection Miracles .. 18.50
Wonder of Guadalupe. *Johnston* 9.00
St. Gertrude the Great 2.50
Mystical City of God. (abr.) *Agreda*. 21.00
Abortion: Yes or No? *Grady, M.D.*. 3.00
Who Is Padre Pio? *Radio Replies Press* 3.00
What Will Hell Be Like? *St. Alphonsus* 1.50
Life and Glories of St. Joseph. *Thompson* 16.50
Autobiography of St. Margaret Mary 7.50
The Church Teaches. *Documents* 18.00
The Curé D'Ars. *Abbé Francis Trochu*. 24.00
What Catholics Believe. *Lovasik* 6.00
Clean Love in Courtship. *Lovasik* 4.50
History of Antichrist. *Huchede*. 4.00
Self-Abandonment to Div. Prov. *de Caussade* 22.50
Canons & Decrees of the Council of Trent 16.50
Love, Peace and Joy. *St. Gertrude/Prévot*. 8.00
St. Joseph Cafasso—Priest of Gallows. *St. J. Bosco* 6.00
Mother of God and Her Glorious Feasts. *O'Laverty* 15.00
Apologetics. *Glenn* 12.50
Isabella of Spain. *William Thomas Walsh* 24.00
Philip II. P.B. *William Thomas Walsh* 37.50
Fundamentals of Catholic Dogma. *Ott*. 27.50
Creation Rediscovered. *Keane* 21.00
Hidden Treasure—Holy Mass. *St. Leonard* 7.50
St. Philomena. *Mohr* 12.00
St. Philip Neri. *Matthews*. 7.50
Martyrs of the Coliseum. *O'Reilly*. 21.00
Thirty Favorite Novenas 1.50
Devotion to Infant Jesus of Prague 1.50
On Freemasonry *(Humanum Genus)*. *Leo XIII* ... 2.50
Thoughts of the Curé D'Ars. *St. John Vianney* 3.00
Way of the Cross. *St. Alphonsus Liguori* 1.50
Way of the Cross. *Franciscan* 1.50
Magnificent Prayers. *St. Bridget of Sweden* 2.00
Conversation with Christ. *Rohrbach* 12.50
Douay-Rheims New Testament 16.50
Life of Christ. 4 vols. P.B. *Emmerich*. (Reg. 75.00) 60.00
The Ways of Mental Prayer. *Lehodey*. 16.50

Prices subject to change.

Prices subject to change.

Practical Comm./Holy Scripture. *Knecht.* (Reg. 40.00) . 30.00
Sermons of St. Alphonsus Liguori for Every Sun. 18.50
True Devotion to Mary. *St. Louis De Montfort* 9.00
Religious Customs in the Family. *Weiser.* 10.00
Sermons of the Curé of Ars. *Vianney* 15.00
Revelations of St. Bridget of Sweden. *St. Bridget* 4.50
St. Catherine Labouré of/Miraculous Medal. *Dirvin* 16.50
St. Therese, The Little Flower. *Beevers* 7.50
Purgatory Explained. (pocket, unabr.) *Fr. Schouppe* 12.00
Prophecy for Today. *Edward Connor* 7.50
What Will Hell Be Like? *St. Alphonsus Liguori* 1.50
Saint Michael and the Angels. *Approved Sources* 9.00
Modern Saints—Their Lives & Faces. Book I. *Ball* 21.00
Our Lady of Fatima's Peace Plan from Heaven 1.00
Divine Favors Granted to St. Joseph. *Pere Binet* 7.50
Catechism of the Council of Trent. *McHugh/Callan.* 27.50
Padre Pio—The Stigmatist. *Fr. Charles Carty* 16.50
Fatima—The Great Sign. *Francis Johnston* 12.00
The Incorruptibles. *Joan Carroll Cruz* 16.50
St. Anthony—The Wonder Worker of Padua 7.00
The Holy Shroud & Four Visions. *Fr. O'Connell* 3.50
St. Martin de Porres. *Giuliana Cavallini* 15.00
The Secret of the Rosary. *St. Louis De Montfort* 5.00
Confession of a Roman Catholic. *Paul Whitcomb* 2.50
The Catholic Church Has the Answer. *Whitcomb* 2.50
I Wait for You. *Sr. Josefa Menendez* 1.50
Words of Love. *Menendez, Betrone, etc.* 8.00
Little Lives of the Great Saints. *Murray.* 20.00
Prayer—The Key to Salvation. *Fr. M. Müller.* 9.00
Alexandrina—The Agony and the Glory. 7.00
Life of Blessed Margaret of Castello. *Fr. W. Bonniwell.* . 9.00
St. Francis of Paola. *Simi and Segreti.* 9.00
Bible History of the Old and New Tests. *Schuster* 16.50
Dialogue of St. Catherine of Siena 12.50
Dolorous Passion of Our Lord. *Emmerich* 18.00
Textual Concordance of the Holy Scriptures. PB. 35.00

At your Bookdealer or direct from the Publisher.
Toll-Free 1-800-437-5876   **Fax 815-226-7770**
Tel. 815-226-7777   **www.tanbooks.com**

Prices subject to change.